"If only I would have known..."

What I wish the Pediatrician would have told me about Language, Literacy, and Dyslexia

Copyright © 2019 by Faith Borkowsky

High Five Literacy Publishing

All rights reserved. No part of this publication may be reproduced, distributed or transmitted in any form or by any means, including photocopying, recording, or other electronic or mechanical methods, without the prior written permission of the publisher, except in the case of brief quotations embodied in critical reviews and certain other noncommercial uses permitted by copyright law. For permission requests, write to the publisher, addressed "Attention: Permissions Coordinator," at HighFiveLiteracy.com

Publisher's Note: This is a work of fiction. Names, characters, places, and incidents are a product of the author's imagination. Locales and public names are sometimes used for atmospheric purposes. Any resemblance to actual people, living or dead, or to businesses, companies, events, institutions, or locales is completely coincidental.

Ordering Information:
Quantity sales. Special discounts are available on quantity purchases by corporations, associations, and others. For details, contact the "Special Sales Department" at HighFiveLiteracy.com

Book Design by Sheryl Lynn Rosenstock Marcus

1st ed.
ISBN 978-1-7340688-0-1

Dedicated to all those parents
 who told me they look back
 with regret –
 that they just didn't know.

Your message has been heard.

Characters

Dr. Allo Graph (Dr. G)

Ms. Query (Mom/Ms. Q)

Dr. Graph

Dr. Allo Graph:
Hello Lex! Good morning, Ms. Query. This visit, I want to discuss Lex's literacy development.

Ms. Query:
Literacy development? He's only four years old!!

Dr. G:
Literacy begins at birth! We are monitoring his language development. Did you or Lex's father have difficulty learning to read?

Ms. Q:
Yes. I always struggled in school, and reading was difficult for me. Why?

Dr. G:
We first look at family history because learning disabilities can run in families.

Ms. Q:
Really? My mother used to say that I just wasn't school material.

Dr. G:
Years ago, we didn't know what we know now about how the brain learns to read. Now, we screen for "literacy health" to detect potential problems and help kids get off to a good start when they enter school.

Ms. Q:
Wow, that's exciting! I was hoping my kids wouldn't have the same struggles I had!

Dr. G:
Let's first look at Lex's speech development. I know he was a late talker, and sometimes that is a red flag for reading difficulties later on.

Ms. Q:
He does have trouble saying certain words, but don't all kids?

Dr. G:
Well, some kids have persistent problems with speech which don't go away without speech therapy. Give me some examples.

Ms. Q:
Lex calls the bathtub a baftub, and he says things like "I go(ed) to school." It's so cute. I'm just so relieved he's talking!

Dr. G:
That's something to keep an eye on. What about rhyming? Do you think he understands rhyming?

Ms. Q:
Maybe, I'm not sure.

Dr. G:
Let's see. Lex, listen to these words. 'Cat' and 'Bat' rhyme. A rhyme is when the endings of words sound the same. 'Pot' and 'Dot' are rhyming words. So are 'Sit' and 'Bit.' Jack and Jill went up the hill.

Dr. G:
Yes, Jill is your sister's name! (Laughing) Listen to the words. Jiiiiiiiiiiilllll Hiiiiiiilllllll. Do they rhyme?

Lex:
Jill and Paige are my sistas! They really big!!!

Dr. G:
(Pointing) Look at these pictures, Lex. This is a cat. This is a hat. This is a ball. This is a bat. Which word doesn't sound like the others?

Lex:
(Points to the cat) Meowwww...

Dr. G:
Could you think of a word that rhymes with 'Cat'? What else has the sound 'at' at the end?

Lex:
Meowwww...

Ms. Q:
Oh boy, I guess not.

Dr. G:
(Pointing to a red circle) Let's try something else. Lex, look at all the pretty colors. What color is this?

Dr. G:
(Pointing to a blue circle)
Very good. What color is this one?

Lex:
Red! (Flapping his wings)

Dr. G:
(Pointing to a blue circle)
You said that one was red. So, what color is this?

Lex:
Red!

Ms. Q:
(Laughing) I guess he likes red!!

Dr. G:
Ms. Query, does Lex remember the names of objects?

Ms. Q:
Some things, yes. When he can't remember, he will call something a "thingy" or say "that whatchamacallit..." He does that a lot.

Dr. G:
(Points to the alphabet on the wall) Lex, look at the letters. Which letter is at the beginning of your name?

Lex:
L!!!! Lex!!!! My name, Lex!!!!

Dr. G:
(Pointing to the E) What about this letter?

Lex:
(Flapping his wings excitedly) Lex!!!

Dr. G:
Ms. Query, does Lex know any of the letters other than L?

Ms. Q:
He knows a few. He sings the alphabet song and mixes up some of the letters, but he is getting there!

Dr. G:
Can Lex retell a story? Does he have a hard time remembering the order of events?

Ms. Q:
He is all over the place!

I'm used to it, but other people can't understand what he's trying to say!

Dr. G:
How about when someone asks him to do something? Can he follow directions? Does he ask you to repeat instructions?

Ms. Q:
Sometimes he remembers the first or the last part but will forget others. And sometimes he just looks confused. He will ask me to repeat the steps over and over again. But boys will be boys... right?

Dr. G:
Well, not really... How are Lex's sisters doing? I didn't ask these questions when they were his age.

Ms. Q:
Jill is 10 years old and Paige is 7. They both have trouble pronouncing words. Jill STILL can't say the word "consonant." She calls it a "continent"! I guess I do, too!

Dr. G:
Hmmm. Did they have trouble learning the alphabet?

Ms. Q:
Not really, but Paige does confuse "U," "W," and "Y." She mixes up the sounds of the letters with their names. Jill writes the letter "b" when she wants to write a "d," and she slows down when reading words with those letters.

Dr. G:
Do Jill and Paige have trouble sounding out words?

Ms. Q:
I don't really see either one of them sounding out words. Jill was always great at memorizing words! She would sit with these little books the teacher sent home and read to the family. I was surprised when she started having trouble reading at 8 years old. Now, she never wants to read, and I can't understand it. Paige tries to sound out words, but she leaves out or adds in sounds that are not there. She reads very slowly and confuses similar looking words such as "then" and "when," "for," "of," and "from," and "saw" and "was."

- then
- when

- from
- of
- for

- saw
- was

Dr. G:
Interesting. How is their spelling?

Ms. Q:
Jill is better than Paige. If she has seen a word, she usually remembers how to spell it. Paige is a very poor speller, and the letters do not always have a connection to sounds. But I just thought that some kids were just bad at spelling... I can't spell if my life depended on it!

Dr. G:
Do they get reading support at school?

Ms. Q:
Oh yes! Jill had one-on-one help for 30 minutes a day, four days a week, for 12 weeks in first grade. In second and third grade, she was seen by the reading teacher in a small group intervention.

Dr. G:
Did the interventions focus on learning phonics systematically?

Dr. G:
When children have trouble reading words and spelling, a program that explicitly shows them how to sound out words is necessary. Sounding out words is called **decoding,** and it is the foundation for all reading.

Ms. Q:
I don't think Jill was taught how to decode words. If she was, I don't think she ever got it. Every week, she came home with a list of words to memorize and those little books in a plastic bag. She did quite well with those books! She would read them over and over again. They had cute pictures that helped her figure out the words and follow the story.

Dr. G:
Unfortunately, it sounds like Jill was not given the right intervention. Memorizing words and using pictures do not really teach a child how to read unknown or hard words. Now that Jill's in fourth grade and the books no longer have pictures or other cues to help her, she's struggling. She really needs to learn to actually read the words accurately and fluently. That will help her forever. What about Paige?

Ms. Q:
I know she receives some phonics at school, but I don't see it working. She has stayed at the same level book the whole year and hasn't made much progress. She seems to have difficulty remembering what she learns. I never see her trying to sound out words at home. She always seems to be just guessing.

Dr. G:
She may need more practice learning how to decode words. It doesn't happen overnight, and there's no quick fix. Paige should be given books that reinforce what she is learning. Otherwise, she will continue to guess at words. I am assuming that writing is also difficult for both Jill and Paige. Is that right?

Ms. Q:
Paige does not hold a pencil correctly, and she does not know how to form letters. She never starts in the right place. I can't wait until the school gives her keyboarding!

Dr. G:
I would not give up on handwriting. Perhaps someone should try teaching her cursive writing. There will be less confusion if she uses connected letters.

Ms. Q:
Boy, I am starting to think that Lex is at risk for reading and writing problems, too. Is there anything I can do with him now?

Dr. G:

Absolutely! Make sure you expose Lex to lots of listening games and books with playful sounds. Read books with alliteration, which are strings of words with the same beginning consonant sound. Kids love to hear Miss Mary Mac! They also love Dr. Seuss books with lots of make-believe words that rhyme!

Ms. Q:

I always loved Dr. Seuss books!

Dr. G:
They are wonderful books. Besides talking and reading to him often, make sure Lex starts to recognize all the letters and knows the corresponding sounds. You can show him how to sound out simple words with short vowel sounds, such as "h-a-t" and "c-a-t." Demonstrate how we read left to right and all through the word by pointing and moving your finger underneath the lines of print. Don't let anyone tell him that he should not use his finger! And to help him with his writing, give him lots of opportunities to play with Play-Doh to strengthen those little fingers! I also suggest giving him little pieces of chalk to help him develop a pincer grip. We want him to learn to hold a pencil correctly.

Ms. Q:
Wow. I will start doing those things. Should I get Lex tested?

Dr. G:
A speech and language evaluation by a speech therapist would be a good start. Find out if universal screeners for dyslexia will be available in the schools. Early identification is so important. In the meantime, you might consider taking the girls to a neuropsychologist.

Ms. Q:
Do you think it's dyslexia, Dr. Graph?

Dr. G:
From the symptoms you described, it sounds like your children's reading and writing problems stem from language-based difficulties. Dyslexia can reveal itself in a number of ways, but the underlying issues are the same; people with dyslexia process language differently, which can make learning to read, write, and spell challenging. As we discussed, children who have problems identifying individual sounds in words and connecting letters to those sounds need the right instruction to learn.

Ms. Q:
What is the right instruction? I have been waiting for someone to teach my kids to read, and it just hasn't happened.

Dr. G:
It can be frustrating. Some children need to learn letter and sound correspondences in a systematic way. The structured phonics approach I mentioned earlier is necessary for children with dyslexia and, quite frankly, it should be used for all children first learning to read. Building a strong foundation through the "right" instruction is right for everyone! Too many kids are struggling in the later grades for this to all be about dyslexia. There's a problem with the way reading instruction is being delivered in the schools. The wrong approach exacerbates language problems that may exist and actually creates problems for kids who otherwise would not have them.

Ms. Q:
I thought maybe they just weren't trying hard enough. Or maybe, they just weren't smart.

Dr. G:
Ms. Query, children with dyslexia try very hard! Many of them work harder than their classmates! You would be surprised how many smart children struggle academically. If you do get an evaluation done, it will give you important information to help advocate for your children.

Ms. Q:
Thank you for the advice, Dr. Graph! I just have a couple of more questions. Lex cannot stand wearing certain clothes and wants me to remove all tags and labels quickly. He seems to be highly sensitive to loud noises and is an extremely fussy eater. Is any of this related to reading and writing or language development? Jill and Paige had many of the same sensory issues, but I never put it together with their learning difficulties.

Dr. G:
It's not always the case, but, frequently, sensory processing and language processing difficulties appear together. Problems with fine and gross motor skills are also warning signs if there are delays or difficulties.

Ms. Q:
One last question! Jill gets distracted in noisy rooms and cannot concentrate. She has trouble completing assignments and easily loses focus in the classroom. And Paige easily gets frustrated and is showing signs of anxiety. Are attentional difficulties connected to reading difficulties?

Dr. G:
Again, it is not unusual to see signs of Attention Deficit Disorder and Hyperactivity in struggling readers. Many children show signs of distractibility along with reading difficulties. And struggling readers are prone to anxiety and low self-esteem. It is hard to feel good about yourself when you always feel ten steps behind your classmates.

Ms. Q:
Thank you, Dr. Graph, for taking the time to explain what I need to watch for in Lex's development. I am determined to not let him fall behind and to get the right help for Jill and Paige.

Dr. G:
You're welcome. Keep me posted.

About the Author:
Faith Borkowsky is the founder of High Five Literacy and Academic Coaching with over thirty years of experience as a classroom teacher, reading and learning specialist, regional literacy coach, administrator, and tutor. Ms. Borkowsky is Orton-Gillingham trained and is a Wilson Certified Dyslexia Practitioner listed on the International Dyslexia Association's Provider Directory. She provides professional development for teachers and school districts, as well as parent workshops, presentations, and private consultations. Ms. Borkowsky is the author of the award-winning book, *Failing Students or Failing Schools? A Parent's Guide to Reading Instruction and Intervention*. She is also a board member of Teach My Kid to Read, a 501(c)(3) non-profit organization with a mission to support and empower students, teachers, and parents through education so all kids, including those with dyslexia, learn to read.

About the Illustrator:
Sheryl Lynn Rosenstock Marcus has been a graphic designer for the past thirty years, a partner in a creative design studio, Wizdom Media, and an author. She is an artist of paint, multimedia, craft, and words.

A note from the Author:

In my private tutoring practice, just about every conversation I have with parents following a reading assessment of their child ends the same way – "If Only I Would Have Known..." Teachers told them their child would be fine. School administrators and educational support team members assured them the right instruction and interventions were being provided. Tutoring centers promised them the moon. Yet, lo and behold, a few years pass, and their child still struggles with reading. I'm constantly reminded of the movie Groundhog's Day, where the same day keeps repeating over and over again. I would always think to myself, "Boy, I could write the script..." And, then I had a thought. "Wait a minute. I SHOULD write the script!"

This "Aha Moment" inspired me to write my *"If Only I Would Have Known..."* series, a set of accessible, graphic plays meant to be read by parents BEFORE they face the heartache of seeking help for their children in a school system that is not working for them. Having been a teacher, reading specialist, regional literacy coach, and administrator, I have seen, firsthand, how schools continue to deliver ineffective reading instruction to the masses, while delaying or denying services to struggling children, many of whom would not be struggling if all children were taught correctly in the first place. I have also heard innumerable accounts from parents who were made to feel as though they were to blame for not adequately preparing their children to learn to read. The truth is there is just too much misinformation coming out of the education community about literacy development in the early stages based upon misguided but entrenched theories of how kids learn to read. Until schools and teaching colleges get on board with the science of reading and there is a paradigm shift in the way reading is taught, it is community members such as pediatricians, preschool teachers, and librarians who will have to be resources for parents concerning effective early literacy development.

In these short, easy-to-understand books, I try to convey the importance of having members of the community support and educate parents early enough in the process to change the trajectory for their children. I provide specific examples of things parents can and should look for to ensure their children get off to a good start when they begin school. My hope is that my *"If Only I Would Have Known..."* series will be made available in pediatricians' offices, daycare centers, preschools, and libraries, as well as in maternity wards, where they can be given as gifts for new parents. If it starts in the community, perhaps the schools and teaching universities will have no choice but to catch on. At the very least, parents will be able to ask the right questions.

www.ingramcontent.com/pod-product-compliance
Lightning Source LLC
Chambersburg PA
CBHW052044070526
44584CB00018B/2605